A Special Day

T0069728

Sally Odgers

Illustrated by Gaston Vanzet

Today is a special day!
Today is festival day.

"It's time to get up," says Mom.

I put on my special clothes.

"It's time to go to town," says Dad.
I pick up my trumpet.

"It's time to start!" says Mr. Cruz.

I play my trumpet.

"It's time to stop," says Mr. Cruz.
I hear the people clap!

12
1
2
3
4
5
6
7
8
9
10
11

"It's time to go home," says Dad.
I say goodbye to Mr. Cruz.

"It's time to go to bed," Mom says.

I say, "Good night."

8:30

Today was a special day.
Today was festival day.